Countries Around the World

Pakistan

Jean F. Blashfield

Chicago, Illinois

www.heinemannraintree.com
Visit our website to find out more information about Heinemann-Raintree books.

To order:
☎ Phone 888-454-2279
🖥 Visit www.heinemannraintree.com to browse our catalog and order online.

© 2012 Heinemann Library
an imprint of Capstone Global Library, LLC
Chicago, Illinois

Edited by Louise Galpine
Designed by Rich Parker
Original illustrations © Capstone Global Library, Ltd.
Illustrated by ODI
Picture research by Mica Brancic
Originated by Capstone Global Library, Ltd.
Printed by China Translation and Printing Company

15 14 13 12 11
10 9 8 7 6 5 4 3 2 1

Library of Congress Cataloging-in-Publication Data
Blashfield, Jean F.
  Pakistan / Jean F. Blashfield.
    p. cm.—(Countries around the world)
  Includes bibliographical references and index.
  ISBN 978-1-4329-5214-3 (hc)
  ISBN 978-1-4329-5239-6 (pb)
1. Pakistan—Juvenile literature. I. Title.
  DS376.9.B56 2012
  954.91—dc22   2010039144

Acknowledgements

The author and publisher are grateful to the following for permission to reproduce copyright material: Alamy pp. 5, 15 (© J Marshall - Tribaleye Images), 13 (© Asianet-Pakistan/ Owais Aslam Ali), 19 (© National Geographic Image Collection/Joel Sartore), 26 (© F1online digitale Bildagentur GmbH/Harald Lueder), 31 (© Fabienne Fossez); AP/Press Association Images p. 37 (Vincent Thian), 8; Corbis p. 9 (© Bettmann); Getty Images pp. 6 (Robert Harding World Imagery/Ursula Gahwiler), 11 (Alex Wong), 16 (Bloomberg/ Asad Zaidi), 23 (AFP Photo/Farooq Naeem), 25 (Daniel Berehulak), 29, 32 (AFP Photo/Asif Hassan), 30 (AFP Photo/Tariq Mahmood), 41 (The Image Bank/Art Wolfe); PA Wire/Press Association Images p. 34; Shutterstock pp. 7 (© Khalilshah), 21 (© Stayer), 33 (© Pichugin Dmitry), 35 (© Monkey Business Images), 39 (© Zotyesz), 46 (© Iakov Filimonov).

Cover photograph of trekkers crossing a swing bridge over the Braldu River en route to Baltoro Glacier, Karakoram Mountains, Pakistan, reproduced with permission of Getty Images (Minden Pictures/Colin Monteath/Hedgehog House).

We would like to thank Lawrence Saez for his invaluable help in the preparation of this book.

Every effort has been made to contact copyright holders of any material reproduced in this book. Any omissions will be rectified in subsequent printings if notice is given to the publisher.

All the Internet addresses (URLs) given in this book were valid at the time of going to press. However, due to the dynamic nature of the Internet, some addresses may have changed, or sites may have changed or ceased to exist since publication. While the author and publisher regret any inconvenience this may cause readers, no responsibility for any such changes can be accepted by either the author or the publisher.

Contents

Some words are printed in bold, **like this**. You can find out what they mean by looking in the glossary.

Introducing Pakistan

Pakistan is both an ancient land and a new country. It is a land of contrasts. It has incredible wealth alongside great poverty. Its people live in bustling cities and remote villages, and they come from many different **ethnic groups**.

Creating Pakistan

Pakistan was carved out of the northwestern and northeastern corners of India when it became independent from the United Kingdom in 1947. Later, the eastern part of Pakistan became a separate country, Bangladesh. The western part is what we now know as Pakistan.

Pakistan is a made-up name. The first part of the name is from the main **provinces** of the country: P is for Punjab, A for Afghania (now called Khyber Pakhunkhwa), K for Kashmir, and S for Sindh. The *-tan* ending comes from the province of Balochistan.

Locating Pakistan

Pakistan is not quite twice the size of California. Iran and Afghanistan border Pakistan to the west. China borders it on the north, while India borders it on the east. The country's coastline is on the Arabian Sea.

Pakistan's population in 2010 was approximately 166 million. It has the sixth-highest population of any nation on earth, but it is only 36th in terms of land area, which means that many people live in a small space. That small space is made even smaller because much of the northern part of the country is covered with towering mountains.

How to say...

"Hello" in Urdu, the national language of Pakistan:
Asslam-o-Alekum (AH-suh-lam-oh-uh-LAY-koom)

Northern Pakistan is a land of rugged, towering mountains and rushing rivers bordering China.

History: Building a Nation

The heart of Pakistan is the Indus River valley. Thousands of years ago, people began to settle in communities there. Over the course of history, the Indus region has been home to many different peoples. New arrivals often came through the Khyber Pass, an ancient trading route through the Hindu Kush Mountains.

Invasions

Followers of Islam, called **Muslims**, arrived soon after the death of Muhammad, its founder, in 632 CE. Islamic rulers and their armies from the city of Mecca, in Saudi Arabia, spread Islam as they conquered a huge part of the Middle East and North Africa. Their **empire** was one of the biggest the world has ever seen. Future Pakistan was just a tiny part of it.

Invaders from Asia founded the Mughal Empire in 1526. This empire spread over what are now both Pakistan and India.

Archaeologists have discovered walls from the ancient city of Mohenjo-Daro in the Indus Valley. The city lasted from about 2600 BCE to 1900 BCE.

The Badshahi **Mosque**, built 300 years ago, can hold 100,000 worshippers.

British rule

British traders first traveled to India seeking to buy and sell valuable spices. In 1858, India became part of the British Empire. Many people who lived in British India were Muslim, but more belonged to a different religion, called Hinduism. Most Muslims lived in the provinces of Punjab, in the northwest, and Bengal, in the northeast.

When India became independent in 1947, the British divided it into a huge Hindu country—India—and a smaller Muslim country—Pakistan. This is known as Partition. Muhammad Ali Jinnah, who had led the fight for a Muslim state, became Pakistan's first leader.

A new nation

Partition had not been handled well, and Pakistan's early years were difficult. Millions of people traveled across the border in one direction or the other. Hindus moved to India, and Muslims moved to Pakistan.

Daily life

Many Muslims moved from India to Pakistan after Partition. They and their children are called *Muhajirs*, meaning **"refugees."** They speak Urdu, the language they took with them. It is now Pakistan's national language.

This photo from 1971, shows East Pakistanis with their belongings fleeing to the Indian border in order to escape the fighting between Bangladesh troops and regular Pakistani forces.

Pakistan itself was made up of two parts, West Pakistan and East Pakistan, which were far apart. A large Indian state called Kashmir was claimed by both Pakistan and India. The two countries went to war over Kashmir in 1947–48. In 1949, the United Nations divided Kashmir between the two countries, but they have never accepted that division. Tensions continue between India and Pakistan.

East Pakistani refugees carry as many belongings as they can, as they flee to the Indian border to escape the conflict in 1971.

Pakistan became an Islamic **republic**, a **democracy** based on religious principles. But the country was torn by violence and conflict. In 1958, President Iskander Ali Mirza declared **martial law** to stop the growing violence, and a military government took over.

It was difficult for one government to control two sections 1,600 kilometers (1,000 miles) apart. In 1971, after a brief civil war, East Pakistan broke away to become an independent nation called Bangladesh.

Daily life

During Pakistan's first two decades, almost one million Muslims moved from Pakistan and India to the United Kingdom. They hoped to escape the violence in their home region, and to find a better life. Today, almost 4 percent of the population of the United Kingdom is Muslim.

Struggling democracy

Pakistan continued to be unstable. In the elections of 1977, Zulfiqar Ali Bhutto's party won, and he became the country's first elected prime minister. But rumors of illegal voting spread, and the military took over again.

Rising extremism

In 1979, the **Soviet Union** invaded Pakistan's neighboring country of Afghanistan. Almost four million Afghans escaped into Pakistan. Some who believed in an extreme form of Islam started a movement called the **Taliban**. In 1996, the Taliban took control of Afghanistan.

On September 11, 2001, **terrorists** attacked the World Trade Center in New York City. An **extremist** group called *al-Qaeda* claimed responsibility. The Taliban had sheltered *al-Qaeda*. The United States and other nations sent troops to Afghanistan to force the Taliban from power and to destroy *al-Qaeda*. The new military leader of Pakistan, Pervez Musharraf, declared that Pakistan was a partner of the United States in the fight.

After international forces invaded Afghanistan, many members of the Taliban moved across the border into Pakistan. The Pakistani army now fights the Taliban throughout Pakistan's **tribal areas**, along the border. Many Pakistanis agree with the Taliban's ideas. Others join the Taliban because it pays them to fight. In 2011 *al-Qaeda* chief Osama Bin Laden was discovered hiding in Pakistan. His death left the situation there even more uncertain.

BENAZIR BHUTTO (1953-2007)

Benazir Bhutto, the daughter of Zulfiqar Ali Bhutto, wanted to restore democracy to Pakistan. She was elected prime minister in 1988. She was the first elected female head of government in the Muslim world. In 2007, she was **assassinated**, and extremist groups that supported *al-Qaeda* were blamed.

Benazir Bhutto, the first female prime minister of Pakistan, was assassinated in 2007.

Regions and Resources: From Mountain to Seashore

Pakistan is a nation of great variety in its land and resources. In the north are mountains capped with **glaciers**, and in the south are the warm waters of the Arabian Sea. In between are broad plains cut by the Indus River.

Mountains

The mountains in the north are part of the Himalayas, the world's highest mountains. Forty of the world's 50 tallest peaks are in Pakistan's northern mountains. They lie in several different ranges that make up the Himalayas. To the east is the Karakoram Range, which has more mountains taller than 8 kilometers (5 miles) than any other range on earth. The Karakoram Highway is the world's highest international paved road. It stretches 700 kilometers (435 miles) from Pakistan into China through a pass at an **elevation** of 4,800 meters (15,750 feet).

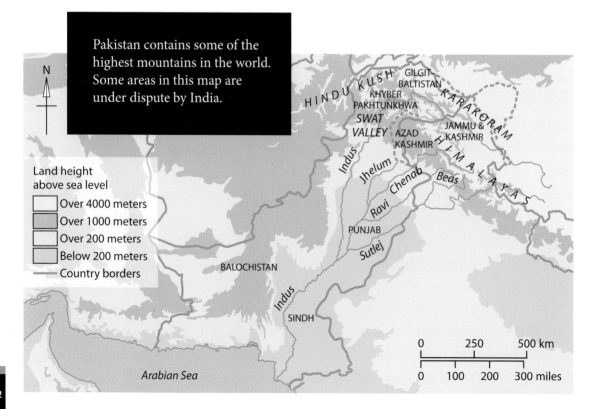

Pakistan contains some of the highest mountains in the world. Some areas in this map are under dispute by India.

To the west is the Hindu Kush, a mountain range that separates Pakistan from Afghanistan. The Swat Valley in the Hindu Kush has been called "the Switzerland of Pakistan" because of its spectacular scenery. It has Pakistan's only ski resort.

In August 2010, Pakistan's worst flooding ever killed hundreds of people and destroyed thousands of villages in the Swat Valley. Around the country, millions of people were left homeless. Flooding may be even worse in the future because climate change is melting Pakistan's glaciers. And without the glaciers, Pakistan and northern India may not have enough water, bringing even greater suffering to the region.

Villagers are stranded by the flood water in Sukkur, Pakistan in August 2010.

Kashmir

The Karakorams border a hilly region called Jammu and Kashmir. After Partition, Pakistan and India fought to control this area, and fighting continues there today. The part controlled by Pakistan is divided into two territories, one called Gilgit-Baltistan and the other called Azad Jammu and Kashmir, or AJK. Since 2009, both of these territories have governed themselves.

Khyber and the tribal areas

From the Hindu Kush southward to Balochistan is a province called Khyber Pakhtunkhwa. Peshawar, the provincial capital, is also the headquarters of the Federally Administered Tribal Area, or FATA. The tribal areas are regions where linked families have much more authority than any government. Altogether, the tribal people make up about 2 percent of Pakistan's population. But millions of them have fled the region, seeking safety from fighting.

Daily life

The tribal areas are not as isolated as they seem. Many men from the tribes are employed as truckers and construction workers. They leave home to work, and when they return, they carry knowledge of the wider world back with them.

The Indus River and Punjab

The Indus River flows through the mountains along Pakistan's northern border. It then travels 2,900 kilometers (1,800 miles) through Pakistan. The Indus dries up during the winter but often floods during the **monsoon** season in late summer.

The name *Punjab* means "five rivers." It refers to the Jhelum, Chenab, Ravi, Sutlej, and Beas rivers, which flow into the Indus. More than half of Pakistan's people live in Punjab. Wheat, cotton, and rice are the region's main agricultural products.

The town of Sust on the Karakoram Highway is a major freight-handling center along the Indus River.

Beautiful woven fabrics are Pakistan's main **export**.

The coast

Two provinces touch the Arabian Sea. Sindh and Balochistan have coastlines totaling 1,120 kilometers (696 miles). Their beautiful beaches draw vacationers. Sindh is the province surrounding Karachi, Pakistan's largest city. Its people make textiles, automobiles, and software, and are involved in entertainment, fashion, publishing, and medical research. The vast western area of Pakistan is Balochistan. It makes up almost half the country's area, but only a small portion of the people live there.

Climate

Winters in Pakistan are usually cool and dry, while spring tends to be hot and dry. Summer is the rainy season, when the monsoon winds carry rain in from the sea. Islamabad, the capital city, gets half its annual rainfall in July and August. The rains gradually lessen through the fall, until the dry winter has returned once again.

Industry and resources

The dry, rocky land of Balochistan provides both oil and natural gas. Oil is found underground in other parts of Pakistan as well. But the country does not produce enough for its own needs. Many Pakistanis use natural gas rather than oil. Karachi has a thriving automobile industry. Pakistani cars run on gasoline or **compressed natural gas** (CNG). Pakistani drivers fuel up with more CNG than any other nation.

Pakistan has a lively movie industry, often called Lollywood. The name comes from combining Hollywood with an L that stands for the city of Lahore, where the industry is based. Like many films made in neighboring India, Pakistani movies are often colorful stories full of song and dance.

Wildlife: Protecting Pakistan's Nature

With its great variety of landscapes and **habitats**, Pakistan is home to a huge range of wildlife. The Indus River draws millions of **migrating** birds every year. They go there from as far away as Africa and Siberia in northern Russia. Altogether, about 660 species of birds live in or pass through Pakistan. Many birds of prey, such as eagles, hawks, and vultures, live there year round.

National Parks

Most of Pakistan's 14 national parks were created to protect specific animals. For example, Khunjerab National Park protects the **endangered** snow leopard and the Marco Polo sheep. These animals were threatened when the Karakoram Highway was built through their habitats.

Lal Sohanra National Park in Punjab is home to several greater one-horned rhinoceroses. These huge mammals live on open grasslands around Pakistan. They are extremely endangered. It is estimated that perhaps as few as 2,700 survive worldwide today.

Chitral National Park in northern Pakistan protects Himalayan black bears, Tibetan wolves, red foxes, and many more creatures.

The spiral-horned markhor, Pakistan's national animal, can be found in many national parks. The markhor is endangered—probably fewer than 2,500 remain. They are found on slopes of mountains that rise to between 600 and 3,600 meters (1,900 and 11,500 feet). Although the name *markhor* means "snake-eating," they do not eat snakes. Instead, they eat grasses on open, rocky land.

The spiral-horned markhor is preserved in many national parks in Pakistan.

Big cats

Many kinds of large cats once lived in Pakistan. The lion, the tiger, and the cheetah no longer survive in Pakistan. But the common leopard is still found in large numbers on the lower slopes of Pakistan's mountains. They prey on rhesus monkeys, which live in the same area. The snow leopard is endangered worldwide, and probably only about 300 of them remain in Pakistan.

In the waters

The Indus River dolphin lives only in Pakistan. About 1,000 of these rare animals survive today. The river where they live has been protected since 1977. These dolphins are unusual in that their eyes see only light and dark. They use echoing sounds to locate prey and to find their way around.

Many other creatures also make their homes in Pakistan's waters, including fish such as risa, loggerhead turtles, yellow-bellied sea snakes, and mugger crocodiles.

Environmental problems

Only 5 percent of Pakistan is forested, and the nation is losing more forest every day. People who live outside cities cut down trees for wood to heat their homes and cook. As forests disappear, so too do the animals and other plants that live there. The government is trying to plant many new trees, but it can't keep up with the tree cutting.

Water resources are also disappearing. The wetlands along the Indus River are drying up, turning more land into desert. This destroys the habitat of the animals that live there. It also means migrating birds can't find a place to rest.

Snow leopards' thick fur keeps them warm, and their large feet help them walk on top of the snow.

Infrastructure: Working for All

Since becoming an independent nation in 1947, Pakistan has struggled to become a democracy. The country's population has vast differences in wealth and education. The influence of the government often does not reach much beyond the cities.

Government

Every Pakistani citizen, male and female, over the age of 18 can vote. Pakistanis vote for the representatives in **parliament**. The members of parliament choose their leader as the nation's prime minister.

Parliament consists of two houses. The National Assembly is the lower house. It has 342 members. The **constitution** calls for 60 seats to be held by women and 10 by non-Muslims. The Senate is the upper house. It has 100 members, 17 of whom must be women. The Senate is elected by the legislatures of the provinces.

Pakistan is divided into provinces and territories. Some areas in this map are under dispute by India.

- Gilgit–Baltistan
- Khyber Pakhtunkhwa
- Azad Kashmir
- Islamabad Capital Territory
- Punjab
- Sindh
- Balochistan
- Federally administered tribal areas

CHINA

Gilgit

Muzaffarabad

Khyber Pass

Peshawar

Islamabad

Rawalpindi

AFGHANISTAN

Lahore • Wagah

Quetta

PAKISTAN

INDIA

IRAN

Hyderabad

Karachi

Arabian Sea

N

0   250   500 km

0   100   200   300 miles

The National Assembly meets in Parliament House in Islamabad.

Education

Public school is required for all children ages 5 to 10. There are public primary, middle, and two levels of high schools. Sometimes, little effort is made to ensure children go to school. Boys average seven years in school. Girls who go to school average six years, but not enough of them attend. Pakistan hopes to achieve equal education for boys and girls. Since 2001, the number of city girls enrolled in school has risen from 43 to 59 percent. In the countryside, the number has risen from 38 to 55 percent.

Pakistan has not put much money into government schools, so every child who can afford to goes to a private school. A child in a village might go to a private school that costs the family only one dollar a year. In a city, they might go to a private school to study in English, use computers, and prepare for college. An estimated 30 percent of school children attended private schools in 2008.

Some children in Pakistan attend religious schools, or *madrassas*. Less than 1 percent of Pakistani children attend *madrassas*.

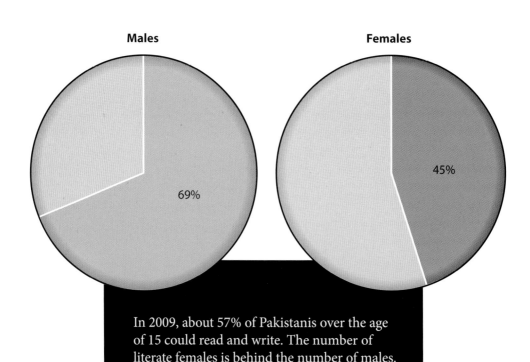

Males

69%

Females

45%

In 2009, about 57% of Pakistanis over the age of 15 could read and write. The number of literate females is behind the number of males.

Boys at religious schools called *madrassas* learn to read the *Qur'an* in Arabic.

YOUNG PEOPLE

Scouting has long been part of life in Pakistan. In 2007, both Boy Scouts and Girl Guides (Scouts) became required in schools, so that young people would be trained to help out in emergencies. There are more than half a million Boy Scouts in Pakistan, but fewer than 100,000 Girl Guides.

The capital

Islamabad has been the capital of Pakistan since the 1960s. It is located at the north end of the Indus Valley. The city was built to be the new capital. It has wide streets and was carefully planned, making it easy for people to find their way around. It has lots of greenery, and a big airport named for Benazir Bhutto. The new Faisal Mosque is the largest mosque in South Asia.

When the city was first built, only government workers moved to Islamabad. Now it has become a popular place to live, with about 700,000 residents.

Government buildings form the heart of the new capital city of Islamabad.

Daily life

Holidays play an important role in the Pakistani culture.

Public Holidays
March 23: Pakistan Day
May 1: May Day
August 14: Independence Day
September 6: Defense of Pakistan Day
September 11: Anniversary of Death of Muhammad Ali Jinnah
December 25: Birthday of Muhammad Ali Jinnah

Muslim Holidays (dates change from year to year)
Ramadan: Ninth month of the Islamic calendar
'Id al-Fitr: End of Ramadan
'Id al-Adha: Feast of the Sacrifice
Muharram: Islamic New Year
Ashura: Day of mourning

Health care

The quality of health care in Pakistan varies widely. Wealthier Pakistanis have good hospitals and doctors. There are 8 doctors for every 10,000 people in Pakistan. That compares with 27 doctors per 10,000 in the United States and 21 per 10,000 in the United Kingdom.

In Pakistan, there are not enough doctors and hospitals in the tribal areas and other rural regions. The Pakistani health care system has trouble serving the huge numbers of refugees there. The refugees often live in poor conditions without access to clean drinking water. Because of this, disease spreads easily.

Culture: Land of Rich Variety

Life in Pakistan's cities resembles life in cities elsewhere. Adults work in offices, children take buses and wear uniforms to school, people watch television at home. In tribal villages, these things often do not happen. There, life is more traditional.

People from many different ethnic groups live in Pakistan. They speak many different languages. The Pashtun people of Khyber Pakhtunkhwa, for example, speak the Pashtun language in cities and small villages. In cities, however, they are more likely to also speak Urdu and English. Although Urdu is the national language of Pakistan, for most Pakistanis, it is their second language.

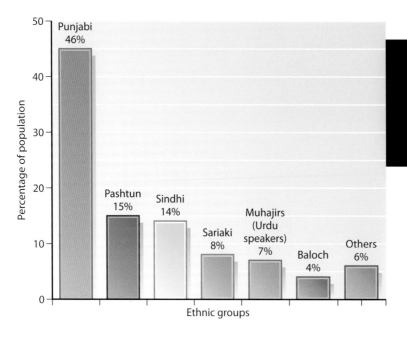

The population of Pakistan is made up of a variety of ethnic groups.

Religion

Most Pakistanis, about 75 percent, are Sunni Muslims, one of the two main **sects** within Islam. The others are Shi'i Muslims. Both groups use the *Qur'an* as their holy book. The **mosque** is the Islamic house of worship. Some cities have hundreds of mosques, while small villages have just one or two.

Daily life

Muslims pray five times every day. Often, they simply stop and pray wherever they are. But at noon on Friday, the Muslim holy day, many people go to the mosque to pray.

Not all Pakistanis are Muslim. The people of Sindhi are Hindus. The Kalash tribe in the Hindu Kush believe in many gods. Pakistan's largest Christian church is St. Patrick's Cathedral in Karachi.

These young men in a Karachi parade are celebrating for *Ashura*, a Shi'i religious holiday.

Women and children

Muhammad Ali Jinnah, the founder of Pakistan, said in 1944: "No nation can rise to the height of glory unless your women are side by side with you; we are victims of evil customs." Soon after that, the wife of the first prime minister started the All-Pakistan Women's Association (APWA). It works to develop women's health, education, and nutrition. She failed in starting female branches of the military, but women became fighter pilots in the military in 2009.

Many traditional Pakistani women will only appear in public wearing a *burka*. This is a robe and headpiece that covers them from head to toe. Not even the face is showing. Other Pakistani women wear a *chador*, a long scarf that covers the head and drapes down over the body.

YOUNG PEOPLE

Girls and boys can play together as young children. But in traditional families, as they near their teen years, childhood friends stop seeing each other. In many families, women and girls leave their homes only with a male family member and only when necessary.

Some women in Pakistan have more freedom than they do in some other Muslim countries. In cities, especially, many women have professional careers. But in more traditional homes it is still regarded as shameful that a woman would need to work.

Young girls in Balochistan wear traditional embroidered clothing.

Both women and men usually wear a *shalwar kameez*. This consists of loose pants and a long top. Women add a matching long scarf, or *dupatta*, for the head and shoulders. Women's clothing is often very colorful with lots of beading and embroidery. Many businessmen dress in Western clothing.

Daily life

Hijab is an Arabic word that means modesty in dress. It is also the name of a scarf that covers the hair, ears, and throat.

Weddings

In Pakistan, most marriages are arranged by the parents of the couple. Sometimes, the bride and groom do not meet before the wedding. A marriage includes several ceremonies. The first is a formal engagement ceremony, during which rings are exchanged and a date is set for the wedding. Other ceremonies involve the exchange of gifts, signing contracts, and the actual wedding ceremony.

A bridal couple brings out their best clothes for their wedding. The long scarf over the bride's head is called a *dupatta*.

Poetry

Most Pakistani art, literature, and music reflects the Muslim faith. That faith has long been expressed in poetry. Muhammad Iqbal (1877–1938) wrote poems about spirituality. His birthday, November 9, is a national holiday in Pakistan.

The owners of cars, buses, and trucks take great pride in decorating them as a way of expressing themselves. The vehicles become moving works of art.

Daily life

Pakistanis usually shop in a local market, or bazaar. People sell fresh foods or products their families have made. Some people lay the goods around them on the ground. Others sell their goods from booths. These kinds of markets are found in both villages and cities in Pakistan. But in cities, people can also go to malls, where they find goods from around the world.

Popular music

Most Pakistani popular music is part traditional and part modern. It is usually sung in Urdu. Among the most popular Pakistani actresses and singers was Noor Jehan (1926–2000). She recorded 10,000 songs and appeared in many movies. Nazia Hassan (1965–2000) was Pakistan's first major pop singer. She died of cancer at age 35.

Sports

Soccer is among the most popular sports in Pakistan. Children throughout the country play it in the streets and fields. Field hockey is Pakistan's national sport. The national team has won four Hockey World Cup titles, more than any other nation. They have also won the Olympic gold medal three times. Pakistan has also been successful at cricket.

Another popular sport in Pakistan is kite-flying. At festivals, fliers sometimes coat their kite string with glass so they can cut another flier's string.

Pakistan's Umar Akmal celebrates beating England in a cricket match in 2010.

Food

The staple food of Pakistan is *naan*. This soft, round bread is eaten at almost every meal. Most meals also include rice, meat, and vegetables. Fruits such as mangoes, apricots, and melons often finish a meal.

Lassi recipe

A popular Pakistani drink is called *lassi*. Try making a mango *lassi* yourself.

Ingredients

- 3½ cup fresh mango, peeled, stone removed, and chopped
- ½ cup sugar
- ¼ tsp ground **cardamom**, rounded
- salt
- 2 cups plain yogurt
- 1 cup ice cubes

Instructions

Mash the mango with the sugar, cardamom, and a pinch of salt until smooth. Add the yogurt and ice and then mash until smooth again. Garnish with a sprig of mint. Enjoy!

Pakistan Today

Since becoming independent in 1947, Pakistan has faced many problems. The country has often been in conflict with its neighbor, India. The Pakistani people have dealt with violence, harsh leaders, and poverty.

Many different groups of people struggle for power in Pakistan today. Some older politicians believe that a few powerful people should be in charge. Others support a more democratic system. The army has great power, but people often distrust it because they feel many army officers are dishonest. Some religious extremists want to remake Pakistan in line with their views. It is not clear which one of these groups will come out on top.

At the town of Wagah, on the only road linking India and Pakistan, crowds gather each day at sunset to watch the border-closing ceremony. It is performed by members of both the Indian and Pakistani armies. For many years, the ceremony threatened to turn violent every night because the two countries were in conflict over the issue of Kashmir. Today, the ceremony is friendlier and less tense. Each day, Pakistanis continue to work to bring peace and democracy to their beautiful but troubled land.

How to say...

"Good-bye" in Urdu:
Khuda-hafiz (koo-DAH-ha-feez)

At one time, the border-closing ceremony at Wagah looked hostile. Now, Indian soldiers (in brown uniforms) and Pakistan soldiers (in black uniforms) are friendlier, and so is the ceremony.

Fact File

Official name: Islamic Republic of Pakistan

Capital: Islamabad

Form of government: Republic

Population: 177,276,594 (2010 estimated)

Largest cities: Karachi, Lahore, Faisalabad

Official language: Urdu

State religion: Islam

Bordering countries: India, Iran, Afghanistan, and China

Area: 796,095 square kilometers (307,374 square miles). This area does not include Jammu and Kashmir.

Major river: Indus

Highest elevation: K2, 8,611 meters (28,251 feet)

Lowest elevation: Arabian Sea, sea level

Currency: Pakistani rupee

Resources: Natural gas, salt, limestone, iron ore

Main imports: Food, petroleum, machinery

Main exports: Textiles, rice, fish, leather goods, chemicals

Main trading partners: China, United States

Literacy rate: 57 percent

Life expectancy: 65 years

Poverty rate: 24 percent

National anthem: "Qaumi Tarana"

Famous Pakistanis: Benazir Bhutto, first female prime minister (1953–2007)

Liaquat Ali Khan, first prime minister (1896–1951)

Muhammad Iqbal, poet and philosopher (1873–1938)

Muhammad Ali Jinnah, founder of the nation (1876–1948)

Pervez Musharraf, military leader and head of state (1943–)

Faisal Mosque in Islamabad is a very modern mosque. It is Pakistan's largest house of worship.

National pride

Pakistan's anthem is known as "Blessed Be the Sacred Land," and it celebrates the faith and glory of the country and its people. It was adopted in 1954.

"Qaumi Tarana"

Blessed be the sacred land,
Happy be the bounteous realm,
Symbol of high resolve,
Land of Pakistan!
Blessed be thou citadel of faith.

The order of this sacred land
Is the might of the brotherhood of the people.
May the nation, the country, and the state
Shine in glory everlasting!
Blessed be the goal of our ambition.

This flag of the Crescent and Star
Leads the way to progress and perfection,
Interpreter of our past, glory of our present,
Inspiration of our future!
Symbol of the protection of God, Owner of Majesty.

Timeline

BCE means "before the common era." When this appears after a date it refers to the number of years before the Christian religion began. BCE dates are always counted backward.

CE means "common era." When this appears after a date, it refers to the time after the Christian religion began.

BCE

4000   Indus Valley civilization begins

CE

711   Islam is introduced to the region.

1526   Invaders from central Asia start the Mughal Empire.

1858   India, including present-day Pakistan, becomes part of the British Empire.

1930   Muhammad Iqbal proposes an independent Islamic state.

1947   Pakistan (with two parts—East and West) are granted independence from India. Pakistan and India immediately go to war over Kashmir.

1949   The United Nations establishes a border between Indian and Pakistani Kashmir.

1958   The military takes over the government.

1970   Pakistan's first general elections are held.

1971   East Pakistan separates from Pakistan to form the nation of Bangladesh.

1973   Zulfiqar Ali Bhutto becomes prime minister.

1979   The Soviet Union invades Afghanistan, and millions of refugees flee to Pakistan.

1988	Benazir Bhutto is elected prime minister, becoming the first female leader in the Muslim world.
2001	General Pervez Musharraf declares himself president.
2005	An earthquake kills tens of thousands of Pakistanis.
2007	Benazir Bhutto is assassinated.
2010	The worst flooding in Pakistani history kills hundreds and leaves millions homeless.
2011	Terrorist leader Osama Bin Laden killed in Pakistan.

K2, the second-highest mountain in the world, rises in the Karakoram Mountains of northern Pakistan.

Glossary

al-Qaeda network of terrorists who were responsible for the 2001 attack on the World Trade Center in New York City and the Pentagon in Washington, D.C.

archaeologist person who studies the remains of past human societies

assassinate to murder an important person such as the leader of a country

BCE means "before the common era." When this appears after a date it refers to the number of years before the Christian religion began. BCE dates are always counted backward.

cardamom seeds of a fruit found in Asia that are used as a spice

CE means "common era." When this appears after a date, it refers to the time after the Christian religion began.

compressed natural gas fuel made from natural gas that is kept under high pressure

constitution written document that contains all the governing principles of a state or country

democracy government system in which people vote for their leaders

elevation height above the level of the sea

empire lands ruled by one country

endangered at some risk of dying out

ethnic group people with distinct, shared cultural traditions

export send goods to another country for sale

extremist someone who behaves in an unreasonable way

glacier slow-moving masses of ice

habitat where an animal naturally lives

literacy ability to read and write

martial law rule by the military

migrate travel to another location, usually covering a long distance

monsoon wind in the Indian Ocean and southern Asia that often carries heavy, unpredictable rain

mosque building where Muslims worship

Muslim person who follows the religion of Islam

parliament group of people elected to make decisions and laws in a country

province region of a country with its own local government

refugee someone who flees their homeland, usually because of war or natural disaster

republic nation in which the supreme power rests with citizens who can vote

sect religious group consisting of members with similar beliefs

Soviet Union country that stretched from eastern Europe across Asia. It broke apart into several smaller countries in 1991.

Taliban group of people who believe in an extreme form of Islam and follow the laws of Islam very strictly

terrorist person who uses violence to try to force change

tribal area part of Pakistan, especially along the border with Afghanistan, where tribes, made up of linked families, have authority

Find Out More

Books

Donaldson, Madeline. *Pakistan* (Country Explorers). Minneapolis: Lerner, 2009.

Heinrichs, Ann. *Pakistan* (Enchantment of the World). New York: Children's Press, 2004.

Kovarik, Chiara Angela. *Interviews with Muslim Women of Pakistan*. Minneapolis: Syren, 2005.

Kwek, Karen, and Jameel Haque. *Pakistan* (Welcome to My Country). New York: Benchmark, 2010.

Mortenson, Greg, and David Oliver Relin, adapted for young readers by Sarah L. Thompson. *Three Cups of Tea*. New York: Puffin, 2009.

Price, Sean. *Benazir Bhutto* (Front-Page Lives). Chicago: Heinemann-Raintree, 2009.

Qamar, Amjed. *Beneath My Mother's Feet*. New York: Atheneum, 2008.

Rengel, Marian. *Pakistan: A Primary Source Cultural Guide*. New York: Rosen, 2004.

Sheehan, Sean, and Shahrezad Samiuddin. *Pakistan* (Cultures of the World). New York: Marshall Cavendish, 2004.

DVDs

Benazir Bhutto: Daughter of Power. NTSC, 2008.

Long Live Pakistan. NTSC, 2007.

Websites

app.com.pk/en_/
Current news in English from the Associated Press of Pakistan.

www.dawn.com/
A Pakistani media site with photos, feature stories, and sports in English.

www.pakistanpaedia.com
An unofficial but complete online encyclopaedia covering all aspects of life in Pakistan.

www.wildlifeofpakistan.com
For information about Pakistan's wildlife and conservation efforts.

Places to Visit

Pakistan Museum of Natural History, Islamabad, Pakistan
The museum collects, identifies, researches, and educates people about plants, animals, fossils, and rocks and minerals resources of Pakistan.
http://www.pmnh.gov.pk/

National Museum of Pakistan, Karachi, Sindh, Pakistan
Exhibits detail archaelogical finds, manuscripts, and historical records of Pakistan.
http://www.caroun.com/Museums/Pakistan/NationalMuseumofPakistan.html

Shalimar Gardens, Lahore, Punjab, Pakistan
Gardens that date back to the Mughal Empire contain marble palaces, decorated mosques, waterfalls, and beautiful gardens.
http://www.lahore.com/
http://mughalgardens.org/html/shalamar.html

Lahore Zoo, Lahore, Punjab, Pakistan
One of the oldest zoos in the world, it houses close to 950 different animals including black bears, lions, and rhinoceroses.
http://www.lahorezoo.com.pk/

Museum of Geological History, Quetta, Balochistan, Pakistan
The museum offers exhibits of geological discoveries in Pakistan.
http://www.gsp.gov.pk/museum/index.htm

Topic Tools

You can use these topic tools for your school projects. Trace the flag and map on to a sheet of paper, using the thick black outlines to guide you, then color in your pictures. Make sure you use the right colors for the flag!

In the Pakistani flag, the green stands for prosperity, and the white for peace. The crescent and star are common symbols of Islam.

N

Islamabad

Index

Titles in the series